VERMONT
FROM
A TO Z

BY JUDSON J. CONNER
Illustrations by Jeff Kaufman

THE NEW ENGLAND PRESS
Shelburne, Vermont

For additional copies or for a catalog of our books, please write:

The New England Press
P.O. Box 575
Shelburne, Vermont 05482

VERMONT
FROM
A ᵀᴼ Z

A STANDS FOR *AYUH*, a word much prized by Vermonters for a variety of reasons. First of all, it can only be pronounced properly by someone possessing a set of Vermont nasal passages. It also appeals to Vermont frugality since it is short and can be uttered equally well inhaling or exhaling. Best of all, it is entirely noncommittal.

Ayuh frequently denotes general agreement, but not necessarily. It can also mean "I heard you," "I am thinking about it," "Just as I thought," "So?," and a whole host of other things, to include nothing at all.

Its use is largely a mystery to outsiders, but Vermonters instinctively understand what is meant by the word in any given situation. Thus, Vermonters are able to carry on lengthy and significant conversations using only that one word, *ayuh*.

B IS FOR BARN. Barns are buildings used to house critters and fodder, normally appearing in shades of red or white and strewn artfully around the countryside to enhance the picturesque nature of the state. And there are a great number of them.

Barns are found in various states of repair, but regardless of their condition, they are almost always in better shape than the houses that go along with them. This particular phenomenon often comes as a surprise to non-Vermonters, who tend to feel that farmers should have more concern for the comfort and well being of their wives than for their livestock.

But romance has nothing to do with it. It is a question of economics and common sense. An uncontented cow tends to drop its milk production, whereas Vermont farmwives (some of the best in the world) function efficiently whether they are contented or not. Vermonters are not particularly romantic. But they are practical.

C STANDS FOR COW. Cows are important to Vermont and there are a lot of them in the state. When downwind and at a distance, tourists find them charming, and they are the originators of a number of dairy products that enrich the Vermont economy.

Cows also possess a little-known ability that allows them to perform a feat of dexterity far beyond the capability of any other large animal. They can slip between two strands of barbed-wire fencing spaced nine inches apart in order to get from a pasture into a vegetable garden. It is a nonreversible skill, however. Once in a garden, cows begin to resemble elephants and eat or trample everything in the garden. Farmers like cows. Gardeners don't.

D IS FOR DOWSER. Dowsers are individuals who locate underground veins of water with the aid of a freshly cut stick of wood and a mysterious gift bestowed upon them at birth.

Thus far, dowsers have managed to conceal the nature of this gift, not only from the general public, but also from scientific inquiry. Dowsers get paid according to reputation and whether or not the client is another Vermonter. Since Vermonters pride themselves on being very scientific, they do not believe in dowsers. So how can dowsers flourish so widely and conspicuously in Vermont?

The ongoing influx of non-Vermonters into the state is one reason—but only one. In reality Vermonters use dowsers too, because even though they may be scientific, Vermonters are also frugal; and after contemplating the high cost of drilling for water, even the staunchest skeptics are likely to hedge their bets by covertly hiring a dowser to advise them on where to drill. If water is found, they do not broadcast the fact that the location was dowser-directed, but the dowser does.

On the other hand, if they end up with a dry hole, as frequently happens, they are not about to let their fellow scientists know they were stupid enough to hire a dowser to locate it. And you can bet that dowser won't tell anyone either.

E IS FOR *EH?*, which is always in the form of a question and pronounced like the "a" in the word "anger." Others in the northern tier of states and parts of Canada also use the word, but none with the flair and skill of the Vermonter.

The word is normally used to mean, "I didn't hear what you said." But in Vermont it can have three additional meanings. *One:* "I heard you, but I can't believe you had the nerve to ask me such a question, so I am going to give you a chance to reconsider," or *Two:* "I heard your question, but I need some time to think of an answer," or *Three:* a combination of *One* and *Two*, as in the following exchange:

"Paw, when you gonna pay me that ten bucks I loaned you?"

"Eh?"

F STANDS FOR FRUGAL. Vermonters are naturally frugal, a characteristic forged over centuries by harsh winters, rocky fields, and thin soil. And they wear the badge proudly, pointing out that frugality is the mother of efficiency, the big sister of ingenuity, and the first cousin of self-reliance.

But Vermonters resent the slanderous and totally false accusations circulated by certain envious outsiders. For example: Vermont is *not* the only state where disposable diapers are washed. They are also washed in parts of New Hampshire and Maine. Nor is it true that most Vermont marriages take place on Christmas so that husbands can consolidate presents. The bride's birthday is an equally popular choice for a wedding date. Hopefully this will set the record straight.

G IS FOR GENEALOGY. Genealogy is important to Vermonters. Every little Vermont town boasts at least one unofficial keeper-of-the-genealogy who knows where and when everyone was born and, likely as not, where one's parents, grandparents, and various other relatives were born.

This interest in genealogy has nothing to do with pedigree or blueness of blood. Vermonters care nothing for titles. But they are curious about a person's degree of "Vermontness" because this establishes social standing and position in the local pecking order.

All of this is sometimes difficult for non-Vermonters to understand. In Virginia a person is either a Virginian or not. Degree has nothing to do with it. And the same thing holds true in Arizona and Iowa and any other state you can name. Except Vermont. In Vermont, in order to qualify as a full-fledged Vermonter, one has to have all four grandparents and both parents born in Vermont, as well as having been born there oneself. In order to barely qualify one has to be the offspring of at least one Vermonter. In case of a genealogical tie, the one who has spent the longest total time in the state is judged the "Vermontest," which explains the reluctance of a dedicated Vermonter to travel beyond the state borders.

Outlanders who move to Vermont to tend goats and commune with nature may convince themselves and the postal authorities that they are Vermonters, but true Vermonters know better. Yet these newcomers should not despair. With a little luck their great-grandchildren can make the grade.

H IS FOR HILLS. Vermont has a lot of hills. It is said that if Vermont could somehow be laid out flat, it would approach the size of Texas. Even its mountains have hills. And almost all the hills run uphill. Vermont is the only state where you can go from point A to point B, then back to A, traveling uphill the whole journey. The few hills that *do* have a downward slope have all been bought up by conglomerates and turned into ski resorts.

This statewide uphill tilt has a lot to do with the longevity of Vermonters, which is derived from the excellent muscular tone that results from spending a lifetime struggling uphill. It also explains why Vermonters always appear to be leaning forward when they leave Vermont.

However, the old adage about Vermont cows having two legs shorter than the others so they can graze on the steep slopes is false. Those mismatched Vermont cow legs result from the cows bracing themselves against the Vermont winter wind. (See W.)

I STANDS FOR INDEPENDENCE. Vermonters have long been known for their independence. In fact, Vermont's struggle for independence began years before the Revolutionary War when a group known as the Green Mountain Boys was formed to discourage New York State sheriffs from collecting taxes in Vermont. At that time Vermont was considered a part of New York by New Yorkers—and by most other people too, for that matter, including the King of England.

Now, whether the Green Mountain Boys were a bunch of tar-and-feather thugs (as claimed by some) or a band of valiant patriots (as claimed by others) is of no real importance. The fact is, they were successful. To this day no New York sheriff in his right mind will venture into Vermont for any reason at all, much less to collect taxes. When the Revolution broke out, the Green Mountain Boys, having by then run out of sheriffs to bully, happily turned their attention to the British, whom they liked scarcely better than New York sheriffs.

The end of the war brought independence from England as well as from New York, and Vermont became an independent nation—one of only three of these United States to ever have achieved such status. Indeed, it was not until the year 1796, history books tell us, that Vermont joined the newly born United States. Or, according to Vermont history books, vice versa.

J IS FOR JAUNDICED EYE, the thing through which a Vermonter views much of the world. This does not mean, however, that all Vermonters are cynical. After all, most of them also have an unjaundiced eye which takes over part of the viewing, thereby allowing the jaundiced eye to be selective.

With this jaundiced eye Vermonters look at flat-landers, politicians, government officials, an assortment of minor antagonists, and anyone who does not agree with their general philosophy and understanding of how things are and should be. Most Vermonters also have a jaundiced ear to go along with the jaundiced eye, and some have jaundiced tasters, feelers, and smellers.

On balance, this inborn skepticism has served Vermonters well. It may have led to some lost opportunities, but it has also preserved the state from numerous hare-brained schemes that have been adopted elsewhere. It has also virtually eliminated campaign visits by presidential candidates, and this alone makes it a virtue.

K IS FOR KITCHEN, the foremost room in Vermont houses. In fact, in the very early days, it was the only room in Vermont houses. Over the centuries, Vermonters have added bedrooms, dining rooms, parlors, and even bathrooms to their houses. But the kitchen has maintained its primacy.

It is almost always a generous room, large enough to hold a good-sized table and a bunch of sturdy chairs, as well as a stove, sink, work area, and cook. Here the family takes its meals, reads, writes, talks, does homework, gets warm, holds meetings, daydreams, entertains kinfolks, and does its indoor socializing.

Most visitors from out of state only get to see Vermont parlors. Parlors are reserved for ministers, politicians, and outsiders. Dogs, cats, and kids are banned from parlors, and even husbands are allowed in only when there is company. Therefore, parlors are spotless (in order to impress visitors), and they are filled with uncomfortable furniture (so the visitors will not stay too long).

If you are ever invited into a Vermont kitchen, take it for the compliment it is. But remember, this does not necessarily mean you are invited to eat. When the lady of the house starts setting the table for supper, it's time to get up and leave.

L STANDS FOR LACONIC. As previously noted, Vermonters are frugal, and nowhere is their frugality more apparent than in their use of words. It has been suggested that this particular characteristic stems from the harsh Vermont winters and the endeavor of Vermonters to minimize the inrush of cold air which occurs whenever the mouth is open.

This harsh-winter theory is further bolstered by the Vermonters' habit of forming their words well up inside their noses (see N), which further minimizes the time the mouth is open. Whatever the reason, Vermonters tend to be laconic by nature. After all, Calvin Coolidge is a favorite son, and there are those who say he was banished to Massachusetts at an early age for talking too much.

At any rate, always pay close attention when talking to a Vermonter. Miss just one word and you could be missing a large portion of the conversation.

M IS FOR MUD SEASON. Vermont is the only state that has five seasons in a year. The fifth, mud season, is located between winter and summer, taking up several weeks of spring and often delving into summer and winter as well.

Mud season occurs when winter wanes and the air warms up enough to melt the snow and top layer of earth, but not enough to reach the underlying frozen ground. All that beautiful white snow is replaced by ugly black mud. Cars fall into mud-covered potholes, small animals disappear, road commissioners hide, and parents take advantage of mud's discipline-enhancing properties by darkly warning unruly kids, "You'd better behave or I'll throw you into the mud."

A few well-heeled Vermonters who can afford it go elsewhere, and some spend the season at a Vermont resort. Vermont has some really fantastic resort facilities, which the law of supply and demand puts within reach of Vermonters during mud season. However, the majority of the population stays inside and stoically rides out mud season, cheered by the knowledge that it will eventually give way to a glorious Vermont summer—something they have been looking forward to since mid-August.

N STANDS FOR NASAL, as used in the phrases "nasal passage" and "nasal twang." Nasal twang is the Vermont dialect that derives its name from the upper nasal passages where Vermonters form their words. How and why they do this is open to debate. Some claim that long exposure to head colds is the cause, while others hold to the harsh-winter theory noted under *L*.

Whatever its origin, the Vermont nasal twang is remarkable in that, unlike the southern or western drawl, it cannot be duplicated by outsiders, although admittedly there are some from the northern reaches of New Hampshire and Maine who come pretty close. Thus, the dialect is frequently used by Vermonters as a recognition signal to keep impostors at bay.

Unfortunately, the corrupting influence of radio and television has seriously eroded the classic Vermont nasal twang, and today there are large numbers of Vermonters who do not use (or in some cases are incapable of using) the dialect at all. Only recently has this alarming trend been seriously addressed. Currently there is a minor movement afoot in the state legislature to require nasal-twang teaching in all elementary schools. But until there is a majority of enlightened lawmakers to make this a reality, we can only pray the endangered nasal twang will somehow hold out and not go the way of the once-numerous Lake Champlain fur walrus.

O IS FOR OUTASTATER, also known as "Flat-lander" or "Furener" or "Alien." An outa-stater is anyone who is not a Vermonter, such as a New Yorker or a Californian or someone from Outer Mongolia.

Contrary to popular opinion, Vermonters like outastaters very much and always go out of their way to extend them a large welcome. After all, it is the outastaters who spend all that money when they come to ski on those downslope hills, and gaze at the cows and barns, and breathe all the nice clean Vermont air, and buy up all the fancy-grade maple syrup.

Of course, Vermonters would just as soon see these outastaters go home after spending their money and a decent period of time in the state, but large numbers of them stay and put down roots, thereby enriching the state in a countless number of ways—and changing it in a countless number of ways.

P STANDS FOR PONDER. Vermonters have developed pondering to a fine art. The trick is to wrinkle the brow, purse the lips, and slowly nod the head while looking off into space. This gives the impression of deep thought.

Sometimes Vermonters who appear to be pondering really are. The very process of using a minimum amount of words requires a certain amount of serious selective consideration. But Vermonters can ponder without really exercising the thought process at all.

This ability explains why so many Vermonters are successful when they seek their fortunes outside the state. In those outlying areas, particularly in Washington, D.C., people who appear to think before they speak are a great rarity indeed, and they give the impression they are very wise. Thus Vermonters always appear much smarter than they really are, and non-Vermonters tend to propel them into positions of authority and power.

Take the presidency, for example. In terms of per capita production, Vermont leads all other states in producing presidents—two of them to be exact. Historians may not cite Presidents Chester Arthur and Calvin Coolidge as having been mental giants, but you can bet they were great ponderers.

Q IS FOR QUEBECOIS. These are Vermont's French-speaking neighbors to the north who live in the Canadian province of Quebec. From them Vermont has derived much of its cultural heritage, a lot of colorful place names, and an abundance of tourist dollars.

Vermonters have always had a warm spot in their hearts for the Quebecois since they are the only ones who come south to winter in Vermont—which tells you something about those Quebec winters. They also come south in the summer, and years ago one would find on weekends and Canadian holidays an occasional Canadian flag floating over a Vermont business establishment to let the visitors from the north know that someone therein spoke French.

Today you will find Canadian flags flying all over Vermont. This does not mean that Vermont merchants all speak French, but rather that Vermont merchants noticed that Canadian tourists made it a point to stop at establishments flying Canadian flags. Nowadays all that flag means when it appears over a Vermont motel or store is that someone therein is happy to accept Canadian dollars. Nor should the Quebecois assume their money is accepted only at establishments flying their flag. They are welcome to spend their money anywhere in Vermont.

R STANDS FOR ROAD COMMISSIONER. The office of Road Commissioner is an elective town office which carries with it very little pay, but an enormous amount of power.

Road commissioners tend to disappear (along with the town roads) during mud season, but the rest of the year they can be found swaggering about town accepting the respect of their fellow citizens. And they receive a great deal of respect, for although road commissioners are not universally loved, they are universally feared.

All this comes about from the fact that in addition to being responsible for filling potholes and removing snow from the town roads, road commissioners get to determine the sequence in which the roads get plowed and the potholes filled. Since the town fund allocated to filling potholes normally runs out long before the potholes do, and since there are degrees of road plowing ranging from complete to none-at-all, and since the time-lapse between the beginning of a snowstorm until all the town roads are plowed is frequently measured in days rather than hours, road-commissioner decisions affect everyone in town. And road commissioners tend to have excellent memories, enabling them to remember who voted for whom at the town meeting. Anyone who owns an automobile or puts any value at all on personal mobility is very careful not to vote for the wrong man.

S STANDS FOR SYRUP. Each spring great quantities of maple syrup are lovingly prepared throughout the state. The syrup is then placed in containers that show the grade and proclaim to the world that this is Pure Vermont Maple Syrup.

Each container is carefully sealed with a seal provided by the Vermont Department of Agriculture, which keeps a wary eye on the proceedings. Although it may add a few pennies to the price of the syrup, this quality control is well worth the price because it provides a very important protection for consumers, particularly out-of-state consumers. It assures them that they have not been hoodwinked into buying an inferior brand of syrup derived from the sap of a tree growing in New York or New Hampshire. (Vermonters, of course, can tell by taste which side of the border the contributing tree was on.)

Tourists should also note that Pure Vermont Maple Syrup comes in various grades. At one time the grading system, according to the degree of lightness and delicacy, was: Fancy, Grade A, Grade B, Grade C, etc. Vermonters tended to eat the Grade C, etc., and sell the rest in order to accumulate foreign exchange. But the full potential of the product could not be realized so long as Grade B was considered inferior to Grade A, as Grade B of anything obviously is.

Vermont ingenuity stepped in to rectify the situation some years ago by changing the grading system to Fancy, Grade A Light Amber, Grade A Medium Amber, and Grade A Dark Amber. It is true that the new Grade A Dark Amber looks and tastes a lot like the old Grade B syrup, but in case anyone has doubts, check the price. That Grade A Dark Amber carries a Grade A price.

T STANDS FOR TOWN MEETING. This is New England's contribution to participatory democracy, and Vermonters take it very seriously. Here they gather once a year to elect road commissioners, reward deserving public officials, throw rascals out of office, and solve all problems, large and small, ranging from cow droppings on public roads to the threat of nuclear war.

More than one Vermont town has solved the latter problem by unilaterally clearing from its premises all nuclear delivery systems and declaring itself a nuclear-free zone, thereby ridding itself of a nagging worry and providing insight into how Vermonters view their place in the world.

There are those who scoff, of course, but proponents of the declaration smugly point out that not a single nuclear-free Vermont town has been hit by a nuclear bomb. In fact, the foreign relations committee of one town was so encouraged by the results that it proposed extending the ban to include conventional weapons. The measure, when it came to a vote, was soundly defeated by a bloc of deer hunters. Nuclear-tipped rockets are one thing, deer rifles quite another.

U IS FOR UNITY. Unity is not a word normally associated with Vermonters, because a Vermonter is just about the most independent creature you will find anywhere on the face of this earth. For two or more of them to be united on any given issue is a rare thing indeed.

Nevertheless, the word unity is part of the Vermont state motto. Seeing it emblazoned there on the state flag is almost like seeing the word "mercy" on the banner of Genghis Khan. But contrary to popular belief, there is one thing that unites all Vermonters: All Vermonters are convinced that the only worthwhile place to live in the whole world is among the Green Mountains.

Unlike Texans, Vermonters seldom talk about the virtues of their state. They figure anyone who has been to Vermont already knows about them. And as for those who have not yet been there? Well, there are enough outastaters cluttering up the place already.

V STANDS FOR VERMONT, a collection of summer greenery lying gently between Lake Champlain and the Connecticut River. Rich in history, its first governor was Thomas

Chittenden (1778); first European, Samuel D. Champlain (1609); first inhabitants, Adam and Eve (years and years, B.C.).

W IS FOR WINTER. This is the season that comes between autumn and mud season and lasts anywhere from six to eight months. Great gobs of snow blanket the mountainsides and howling winds rush down from the North Pole to frostbite ears and blow over cows.

Except for a few ice fishermen and those connected with the ski industry (such as plastic surgeons), true Vermonters don't like winter, and they go to great pains to avoid going out in it. A few of the old timers have learned to hibernate, which accounts for the dramatic drop in Vermont mortality rates during the winter months.

This phenomenon was long thought by the outside world to stem from a conspiracy among Vermont coroners to avoid digging graves while the ground was frozen. But this is not so. It is caused by hibernation. One has to wait for the return of warm weather to see if Great Aunt Maud is going to wake up.

X STANDS FOR EXTREE. This is the amount over the advertised rate you pay if you want a room with a view of the mountains rather than the rear door of Carla's Cafe and Bar. It is what you pay for the basket if you too readily agree to the asking price for a bushel of apples.

Knowing this, Vermonters are careful not to appear overly eager to buy anything no matter how much they want it. As a matter of course, they protest the posted price as being outrageous and agree to pay it only after much thought and with great reluctance.

This does not necessarily mean they think the asking price is excessive. Rather it is a signal to the seller that they are not going to stand for any "extree" charges being tacked on once they agree to buy. So ingrained is this trait among Vermonters that it is not unusual to see them haggling with a coin-operated machine before buying a can of soda pop.

Y IS FOR YANKEE. Vermont is the home of Yankees. In foreign lands, Yankee is a term applied to all Americans, as in the phrase, "Yankee go home!" In the southern part of the country the word becomes "damnyankee" and there are none of them around. North of the Mason-Dixon line the word reverts to its shorter form, but no one claims to be one. Instead, everyone points to New England as the home of the Yankee.

But even here, those in the southern-most three states point northward. The people of Maine like to think of themselves as "Downeasterners," and the citizens of New Hampshire are too busy building tourist roads through the White Mountains to think of themselves as being anything in particular. Thus, it is only in Vermont that you find anyone who will admit to being a Yankee.

Vermonters are proud of the title, and they can't understand that phrase, "Yankee go home!" Why should any Yankee want to be anywhere but home in the first place?

Z STANDS FOR ZERO. When the temperature dips to this point on a Fahrenheit thermometer, Vermonters start feeling chilly. On most thermometers this is a fixed point, but on Vermont thermometers the zero begins to float upward as the winter wears on, thus providing ever lower temperatures for individuals to report to each other following cold nights. At any particular gathering, the last one to render his report normally has the lowest reading. The record, set some years ago at a large meeting, is 219 degrees below zero.